small world
Washing!

Gwenyth Swain

ZERO TO TEN

To find out more about the pictures in this book, turn to page 22.
To find out more about sharing this book with children, turn to page 24.

First published in this edition in Great Britain by Zero To Ten Limited, part of the Evans Publishing Group, 2A Portman Mansions, Chiltern St, London W1U 6NR

Reprinted 2006

Published by arrangement with Carolrhoda Books, Inc., a division of Lerner Publishing Group, 241 First Avenue North, Minneapolis, MN 55401, U.S.A.

A CIP catalogue record for this book is available from the British Library.

ISBN: 1-84089-392-3
13-digit ISBN (from 1 Jan 2007) 978 1 84089 392 2

The photographs in this book are reproduced with the permission of: © Sylvie Villeger/Photo Researchers, Inc., front cover; © Trip/J. Wakelin, back cover, 16; ©Trip/J. King, p. 1; © Trip/Eric Smith, p. 3; © Michael S. Yamashita/CORBIS, p. 4; © Wolfgang Kaehler, p. 5; © Trip/S. Grant, p. 6; © Paul J. Buklarewicz, p. 7; © Elaine Little/World Photo Images, p. 8, 13; © Trip/D. Clegg, p. 9; © Margaret Miller/Photo Researchers, Inc., p. 10; © Trip/H. Rogers, p. 11; © Dean Conger/CORBIS, p. 12; © Fotografia, Inc./CORBIS, p. 14; © Nancy Durell-McKenna/Panos Pictures, p. 15; © Jeanie Woodcock, Reflections Photolibrary/CORBIS, p. 17; © Lawrence Migdale/Photo Researchers, Inc., p. 18; © Trip/David Pluth, p. 19; © Margie Politzer/Photo Researchers, Inc., p. 20; © Trip/J. Dennis, p. 21.
Copyright © 2002 by Gwenyth Swain

Are there days when
you need a good wash?

Did you decide to
slide in something icky?

Did your favourite food
leave you all sticky?

When you need a good wash,
there's no time to waste.

Take a break and jump in a lake.

Turn on the tap. Fill a bucket.

Wash yourself by the nearest well.

Lather up till bubbles fly.

Keep the soap out of your eyes!

Scrub yourself from top to toe.

Be sure to rinse before you go.

Rub down wet skin.

Flash a clean grin.

Part your hair in one neat line.

Comb it. Brush it. Make it shine.

Learn to wash yourself well,

and you can wash others, too.

Some critters need help

doing what you can do.

More about the Pictures

Front cover: A four-year-old girl has fun washing her hair.

Back cover and page 13: A mother pours water from a bucket to rinse off her child in the Philippines.

Page 1: A British boy proudly shows off clean teeth.

Page 3: On a hot day in the UK, a baby takes a bath in a wheelbarrow.

Page 4: A group of Thai children have fun playing in the mud along the Mekong River bank.

Page 5: This boy in Bergen, Norway, discovers that it's hard to eat ice cream without getting *very* sticky.

Page 6: A boy in California, USA, takes the time to wash his hands, making lots of suds with soap.

Page 7: A natural hot spring on the island of Okinawa in Japan makes the perfect outdoor tub.

Page 8: In Manila in the Philippines, two boys rinse off after a bath.

Page 9: A large well in Lombok, Indonesia, is just the spot for a quick wash.

Page 10: A boy in India lathers his hair with shampoo.

Page 11: Soap bubbles make washing fun for this British girl.

Page 18: A girl in California, USA, wipes her face while looking in the bathroom mirror.

Page 12: Boys wash in a communal shower on the island of Java in Indonesia.

Page 19: An older sister washes the baby of the family in a big round bowl in Kampala, Uganda.

Page 14: A father helps his child dry off after a bath.

Page 20: A *mahout* – someone who keeps elephants and trains them to work – helps one of his animals get clean in a river in

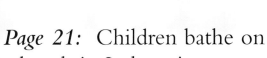

Page 15: Brothers in Calcutta, India, brush their teeth using their fingers.

Do you help your pets stay clean?

Page 16: On the island of Sumatra, in Indonesia, a mother combs out tangles in her daughter's hair.

Page 21: Children bathe on a beach in Indonesia

Page 17: This girl in Britain has a lot of hair to brush!

A Note to Adults on Sharing This Book

Help your child become a lifelong reader. Read this book together, taking turns as you both read out loud. Look over the photographs and choose your favourites. Sound out new words and go back to them later to look at them again. Then try these 'extensions' – activities that extend the experience of reading and build discussion and problem-solving skills.

Talk about Washing
All around the world, people wash themselves in different ways. Discuss with your child the reasons why people wash themselves. Take a closer look at the pictures in this book. In how many different locations and in how many kinds of containers are children shown bathing themselves? How do the ways of bathing differ from your child's usual bath? How are they the same?

Wall of Washing
With your child, gather pictures of people and animals washing. Look through magazines for pictures of people brushing their teeth or animals grooming themselves. Search the newspapers for advertisements for your favourite soap and shampoo – or for your dog's flea bath. Take a camera to the zoo and snap shots of animals cleaning themselves or soaking in pools. Then put all of these pictures on a poster board or on the wall in your bathroom. Ask your child to compare and contrast the ways that animals and people wash themselves.